King
Charles III

Susanna Davidson

Designed by Karen Tomlins

History consultant: Hugo Vickers

Family Tree

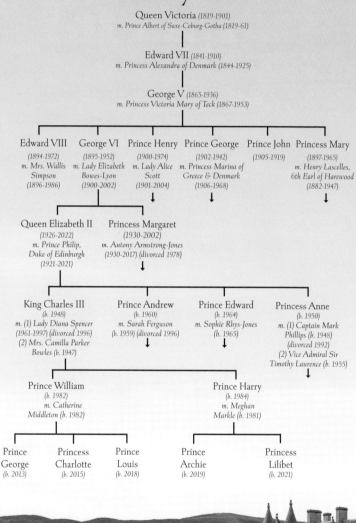

Queen Victoria *(1819-1901)*
m. Prince Albert of Saxe-Coburg-Gotha (1819-61)

Edward VII *(1841-1910)*
m. Princess Alexandra of Denmark (1844-1925)

George V *(1865-1936)*
m. Princess Victoria Mary of Teck (1867-1953)

Edward VIII	George VI	Prince Henry	Prince George	Prince John	Princess Mary
(1894-1972)	*(1895-1952)*	*(1900-1974)*	*(1902-1942)*	*(1905-1919)*	*(1897-1965)*
m. Mrs. Wallis Simpson (1896-1986)	*m. Lady Elizabeth Bowes-Lyon (1900-2002)*	*m. Lady Alice Scott (1901-2004)*	*m. Princess Marina of Greece & Denmark (1906-1968)*		*m. Henry Lascelles, 6th Earl of Harewood (1882-1947)*

Queen Elizabeth II
(1926-2022)
m. Prince Philip, Duke of Edinburgh (1921-2021)

Princess Margaret
(1930-2002)
m. Antony Armstrong-Jones (1930-2017) (divorced 1978)

King Charles III	Prince Andrew	Prince Edward	Princess Anne
(b. 1948)	*(b. 1960)*	*(b. 1964)*	*(b. 1950)*
m. (1) Lady Diana Spencer (1961-1997) (divorced 1996) (2) Mrs. Camilla Parker Bowles (b. 1947)	*m. Sarah Ferguson (b. 1959) (divorced 1996)*	*m. Sophie Rhys-Jones (b. 1965)*	*m. (1) Captain Mark Phillips (b. 1948) (divorced 1992) (2) Vice Admiral Sir Timothy Laurence (b. 1955)*

Prince William
(b. 1982)
m. Catherine Middleton (b. 1982)

Prince Harry
(b. 1984)
m. Meghan Markle (b. 1981)

Prince George	Princess Charlotte	Prince Louis	Prince Archie	Princess Lilibet
(b. 2013)	*(b. 2015)*	*(b. 2018)*	*(b. 2019)*	*(b. 2021)*

Contents

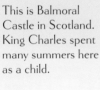

This is Balmoral Castle in Scotland. King Charles spent many summers here as a child.

Chapter 1

A son and heir

It was a bleak and foggy winter. Britain was still recovering from the Second World War, which had only ended three years before. But, on November 14, 1948, people up and down the country were celebrating. Princess Elizabeth, the King's elder daughter, had given birth to her first child, Prince Charles Philip Arthur George. The birth took place at Buckingham Palace, in the Buhl Room, which had been turned into a miniature hospital. As soon as the father, Prince Philip, heard the news he rushed in and gave his wife a bouquet of flowers.

An announcement was posted on the palace railings just before midnight. Crowds cheered and sang outside the palace gates. Meanwhile, the baby Prince was placed in a cot in a huge gilded ballroom, so all the staff could see him. At just a few hours old, Prince Charles' life in the spotlight had begun.

Crowds gather outside Buckingham Palace to celebrate the news of the birth of Prince Charles.

Princess Elizabeth with her baby,
Prince Charles, in his christening robes

Four weeks later, the christening was held in the Music Room at Buckingham Palace. The Archbishop of Canterbury sprinkled the baby Prince with water from the River Jordan, while his family and eight godparents looked on.

Princess Elizabeth was delighted with her baby but, with royal duties to attend to, she was often apart from him. When Prince Philip, who was in the Royal Navy, was posted to Malta in October 1949, Princess Elizabeth left Charles to be with him.

The young Prince was mostly looked after by his nannies. The first, Helen Lightbody – known as "No Nonsense Lightbody" – arrived when Prince Charles was just a month old. She was eventually dismissed, however, after Elizabeth decided she was too strict with the children.

Charles was very close to his other nanny, Mabel Anderson. He later described her as "warm, loving, sympathetic and caring" and she stayed with the royal family for thirty-two years. Even after she retired, she often spent Christmases with them.

In August 1950, Prince Charles became a brother, when Princess Elizabeth gave birth to her second child, Princess Anne.

Princess Elizabeth adored the time she had with her young children. People said that she always looked forward to "Mabel's night off" when she could enjoy bathing her children,

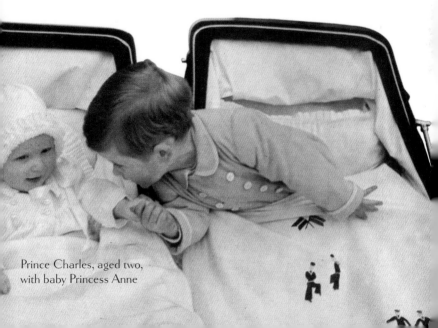

Prince Charles, aged two,
with baby Princess Anne

reading to them and putting them to bed.

From the start, Charles and Anne had very different personalities. Whereas Charles was often shy and sensitive, Anne was much more confident and outgoing, like her father. But they were very close, spending much of their time together in the nursery. Years later, Charles remembered how they would garden together: "My sister and I had a little vegetable patch in the back of some border somewhere... We had great fun trying to grow tomatoes rather unsuccessfully and things like that."

Charles and Anne were to see even less of

their parents after the death of their grandfather, King George VI, on February 6, 1952.

At the age of just twenty-five, their mother became Queen – not only of the United Kingdom, but also other Commonwealth realms.

Charles' grandfather, King George VI, in 1950

8

Despite being a young wife and mother, she had to put royal duties first, now more than ever.

The Coronation was planned for June 2, 1953 and from this time on, Charles had to learn that his mother was also the Queen. He has a vivid image from this time, of his mother coming into the nursery at bath time, dressed in the extremely

Queen Elizabeth II at her Coronation, wearing the Coronation robes and crown

heavy St. Edward's Crown, in preparation for her Coronation.

For the Coronation day itself, Charles was dressed in a white satin shirt and long white trousers, his hair thick with lacquer to keep it looking neat. The Prince sat beside his grandmother, now the Queen Mother, and his aunt, Princess Margaret, for the three-hour service. At just three years old, Charles had become first in line to the throne.

Prince Charles, standing between his grandmother, the Queen Mother, and his aunt, Princess Margaret, at the Queen's Coronation at Westminster Abbey on June 2, 1953

Prince Charles with his beloved grandmother in April, 1954

The young Prince had a very loving relationship with his grandmother, the Queen Mother. She was always affectionate and encouraging and shared with him her love of music and art. He later described her as, "quite simply the most magical grandmother you could possibly have" and they always remained very close.

From an early age, Charles had a passion for the natural world. Every summer, the family would head to Balmoral Castle, in Scotland, where his father took him shooting and fishing, and his mother taught him to ride a horse. He loved his time, too, at the family estate in Sandringham, Norfolk, where they would all spend Christmas.

At first, Charles was taught at home by a governess, Catherine Peebles – known to him as "Mispy" – but his parents decided that Charles should start mixing more with other children. At the age of eight, he became the first heir to the throne to be educated outside of the palace. For six months, Charles went to Hill House School in London, arriving on his first day in a royal limousine.

The royal family outside Balmoral Castle, in September, 1960

His first-term report praised his reading and writing, although described his mathematics as "careful but slow, not very keen."

After just six months at Hill House, however, Charles was sent to Cheam, a boarding school in Berkshire.

A sensitive child, Charles found living away from home very hard.

Charles, with his headteacher, outside Hill House School

An action shot of a young Prince Charles, playing cricket for Hill House School in July, 1957

Prince Charles arriving at Cheam School in September, 1957, and meeting the headteacher, Peter Beck

He became homesick and would hug his teddy bear for comfort at night. He also struggled to make friends and fit in, although his headteacher described him as a very hardworking and able boy, and praised his written work.

The Queen knew her son was unhappy. In a letter to the Prime Minister, Anthony Eden, in 1958, she wrote: "Charles is just beginning to dread the return to school next week – so much worse for the second term." But the Queen left most of the decisions about the family to Prince Philip, who believed Charles needed these experiences to prepare him for royal life.

It was at Cheam, at the age of nine, that Charles first discovered that he had been made Prince of Wales. He was watching the closing ceremony of the Commonwealth Games on television in the headteacher's study, with a group of other boys, when

Charles, aged 11, two years into his time at Cheam

the Queen appeared on screen with a pre-recorded message, announcing: "I intend to create my son, Charles, Prince of Wales today."

The other pupils turned to congratulate Charles but he later described the "horror and embarrassment" he felt at that moment.

When Charles left Cheam, his grandmother hoped he would go to Eton College, near to Windsor Castle, one of the royal homes. But Prince Philip was determined his son should go to his old boarding school, Gordonstoun, on the north-east coast of Scotland. "He might as well be at school abroad…" the Queen Mother wrote to the Queen, but there was nothing she could do to change their minds.

15

Prince Charles gets on the plane to fly to
Gordonstoun with his father, in 1962.

Chapter 2

Far from home

Prince Philip, a qualified pilot, flew his son up
to Scotland for his first term at his new school.
Prince Philip had loved his time at Gordonstoun
but from the start, Prince Charles felt that the
school was like a prison sentence.

The headteacher believed it was important to build up his pupils' character through physical challenges, which included ice-cold showers and a run every morning. The boys had to wear shorts, even in the winter, and sleep with open windows in the dormitories all year round. Some mornings, the pupils would wake up with snow on their beds.

But it was the bullying that really got to Charles. From the start, the other boys ignored him, as they

Prince Charles, next to his father, arrives at Gordonstoun school.

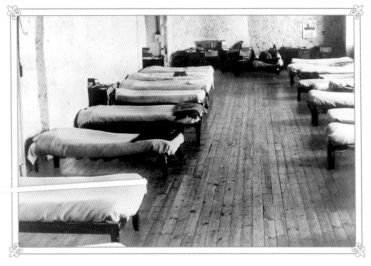

A dorm room at Gordonstoun School, in 1962; the boys were expected to make their own beds and polish the dormitory floor.

didn't want to look as if they were sucking up to him, but the nights were the worst. "I hardly get any sleep..." he wrote to his mother, "because I snore and get hit on the head the whole time. It's absolute hell."

Charles withdrew into himself and became even more shy. "I wish I could come home..." he wrote again, in his second year. The Queen thought about letting Charles leave, but Prince Philip, believing he was doing what was best for his son, wanted Charles to stay. He wrote back, urging Charles to be strong.

While at Gordonstoun, Charles discovered his love for drama, playing the title role of Macbeth, and the Pirate King in *The Pirates of Penzance*. However, he didn't share his father's talent for rugby or cricket and he was longing to prove himself physically. So when Prince Philip decided to send his son to Australia, at the age of seventeen, Charles leaped at the challenge.

Charles at Timbertop School, Australia, in February, 1966, using a bush saw to fell a tree.

He went to Timbertop, a school in the wilderness of the Australian outback. Unlike Gordonstoun, Charles wasn't bullied at Timbertop, and he threw himself into long hikes in the boiling heat, cross-country runs and wood splitting. The headteacher said he was an admirable leader in charge of younger boys.

For the first time, the Prince faced the crowds that had gathered to meet him on his own. "I took the plunge and went over and talked to people... That suddenly unlocked a completely different feeling and I was then able to communicate and talk to people much more."

Smiling crowds gather to greet Prince Charles at Bondi Beach, Australia, in May, 1966.

Charles would remember his time at Timbertop as the most enjoyable part of his whole education. He returned to Gordonstoun more confident and was made Head Boy for his final year.

The struggles and the loneliness that Charles faced at Gordonstoun would stay with him for life. Later, however, when thinking back over his time there, he said it had taught him to accept challenges and take the initiative.

As with all the other decisions about Charles' life, the next one was made for him by his parents, along with a committee which included the Prime Minister and Charles' great-uncle, Lord Mountbatten. They decided Charles should head to Cambridge, one of Britain's top universities.

Prince Charles, in his academic robes, arrives for his first term at Cambridge University in October, 1967.

Prince Charles, aged 22,
playing polo at Windsor

Charles' life at Cambridge wasn't quite that of a
normal student. He was given special rooms, for
which the Queen ordered carpets and curtains
to make them more comfortable, and the Queen
Mother added a painting by one of her most-loved
artists. He had a private bathroom built for him,
too, and rooms were also provided for Charles'
staff, who managed his appointments.

Charles chose to study anthropology and
archaeology in his first year, and worked hard.
In his free time, he enjoyed playing polo, a
fast-paced game on horseback with wooden

mallets, and joined a drama group. However, much of his time was taken up with duties, which interrupted his learning. This included going to Australia, for the Prime Minister's funeral, as well as two trips to Malta.

Charles rehearsing a sketch at Cambridge University

Even more overwhelming was the upcoming ceremony, known as the "Investiture" – when Charles would be formally presented to the Welsh people as their Prince. It was to take place on July 1, 1969, at Caernarfon Castle, in Wales, in front of 4,000 guests, as well as being broadcast live on TV to millions.

In order to prepare for it, Charles was sent to a university in Wales for nine weeks, to learn the Welsh language and about Welsh history and culture. At the time, more and more Welsh people were demanding independence for Wales, and the royal family was becoming less popular. It was hoped that Charles' visit would help change that.

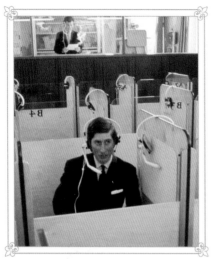

Uprooted once again, the Prince found it a lonely time. "Every day," he said, "I had to go down to the town where I went to these lectures, and most days there seemed to be a demonstration going on against me." But he worked

Prince Charles, in April, 1969, learning Welsh at Aberystwyth University's language laboratory

hard and grew to love the Welsh language and to care deeply about the Welsh people.

Before the end of the term, he gave a speech, in Welsh, at a Welsh youth festival. Charles carried on speaking, even as protesters entered the hall, waving banners and calling for Welsh independence. They were made to leave and Charles carried on calmly. On finishing, he was met with cheers and a huge round of applause.

On the day of the Investiture itself, Charles was filled with nerves. Extra police officers had to be called in, because of fears of violence from

Welsh nationalists. Charles entered to music, then strode towards the stage, kneeling on a scarlet cushion before his mother. The Queen handed him the symbols that marked him as Prince of Wales: a sword, a coronet, a gold ring, a gold rod and a cloak, known as a kingly mantle.

At the Investiture ceremony at Caernarfon Castle, Wales, Prince Charles holds hands with his mother, the Queen.

Then Charles placed his hands between hers and made an oath: "I, Charles, Prince of Wales, do become your liege man of life and limb and of earthly worship, and faith and truth I will bear unto thee to live and die against all manner of folks." He later said he found this the most moving and meaningful moment.

Charles followed up his Investiture with a tour of Wales and was touched by the cheering crowds that came to meet him.

After the summer, he returned to Cambridge for his final year of university. That November, 1969, Charles had his twenty-first birthday. There was a grand party at Buckingham Palace with more than 400 guests, a feast of melon, lobster, pheasant and champagne, followed by a concert, fireworks and dancing.

Becoming twenty-one meant Charles also gained access to a new source of wealth – the Duchy of Cornwall, which included thousands of acres of farmland and property in London, as well as quarries and mines. But no amount of wealth or lavish parties could distract Charles from the serious issues he cared about.

In 1970, three months after leaving Cambridge,

he gave his first speech on the environment, at Bangor University, in Wales. He spoke about the dangers of pollution, as well as about the worrying mountains of plastic waste.

Prince Charles in Snowdonia, where he walked with other members of the Countryside Steering Committee for Wales, after giving his first speech on the environment.

One of Prince Charles' paintings of the Scottish landscape, "Kilphedir Pool on River Helmsdale, Sutherland"

Charles' passion for nature was made even stronger by his love of outdoor painting. He found it soothing – a way to refocus his energies. "It all requires the most intense concentration," he said, "and, consequently, is one of the most relaxing and therapeutic exercises I know."

Charles' education had been very different to previous heirs to the throne. He was the first to complete a university degree and he'd had to try to live the life both of a royal and an "ordinary" person. It had been difficult and it had been lonely, but it had taught the Prince to question and challenge himself, and to form his own opinions. Moreover, he had begun to show he wasn't afraid to speak out about the things that mattered most to him.

Chapter 3

Army life

After university, Charles and his sister, Anne, enjoyed working as a team, representing Britain abroad. They were close in age compared to the Queen's third and fourth children – Prince Andrew, born in 1960, when Charles was 11, and Prince Edward, born in 1964.

A photo of the royal family in April, 1965, with baby Prince Edward in white, watched by their mother, the Queen, as well as Princess Anne, Prince Charles, Prince Andrew and their father, Prince Philip.

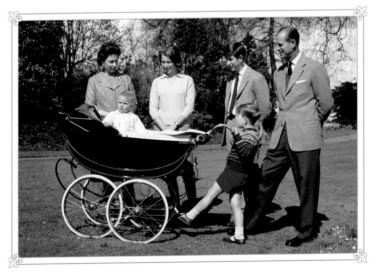

The large age gap meant that Charles and Anne were often apart from their younger siblings as they were growing up. By the time Charles left university, the whole family was still living together at Buckingham Palace. The Queen and Prince Philip had private apartments on the north side of the palace, while Prince Edward's rooms were on the floor above, along with his nannies. Prince Andrew was away at boarding school and Princess Anne divided her time between her career with horses and her royal duties.

Charles was growing close to another family member – Lord Mountbatten, known as "Uncle Dickie" to the family, whom Charles thought of as a grandfather figure.

Mountbatten was the younger brother of Prince Philip's mother, Princess Alice. Charles loved to visit him at his estate, Broadlands, and would talk to his great-uncle for hours, often turning to him for advice.

Mountbatten, along with Prince Philip, encouraged Charles to take a course in the RAF (Royal Air Force) after university. And so, in March 1971, nine months after graduating,

Here, Prince Charles is about to have a flying lesson at the RAF college in Cranwell. The photo was taken in March, 1971.

Charles found himself at an RAF base in Lincolnshire, learning how to fly.

It was a tradition in the royal family for the men to do military training and, once Charles had learned to fly jet aircraft, he was enrolled on yet another course, this time at the Royal Naval College.

The Prince, in training with the RAF, makes his first parachute jump in Poole, Dorset, in July, 1971.

Both Prince Philip and Mountbatten had done extremely well in the Navy, with Mountbatten serving as First Sea Lord, so Charles had a lot to live up to. He wrote to Mountbatten about his struggles and his feelings of hopelessness.

Even if the Navy wasn't easy for Charles, he didn't give up. For five more years, he served on two frigates, HMS *Minerva* and HMS *Jupiter*. The *Minerva* captain commented on the way the Prince always looked out for his fellow seamen.

After his time on HMS *Jupiter*, Charles trained to fly as a helicopter pilot and joined the Naval Air Squadron aboard HMS *Hermes*.

You can just make out Prince Charles at the controls here, about to take off at a Royal Naval Air Station.

A sixteen-year-old Prince Andrew stands beside his brother, Prince Charles, aboard the minesweeper Charles was commanding, the HMS *Bronington*, off the coast of Scotland.

By the end of his service, Charles was commanding a minesweeper. He was praised in his final report for keeping up the spirits of the sailors and for his professional approach. But with the end of his career in the Navy came the big question – what should he do with his life?

By now, the Prince had many interests and passions. He loved playing polo, painting, fishing, skiing and foxhunting. He was often abroad on royal visits and was just as happy to spend an evening at home, reading about history or philosophy. But it wasn't enough to fill his life.

The trouble was, as heir to the throne, Prince Charles had no clear job. Instead, as he later remarked, there was the need to make it up as you went along. The Prince knew that he might not become king for forty years, and in an interview in 1969, he revealed, "I don't want to be a figurehead. I want to help get things done."

And so in June 1976, with the money he received when he left the Navy, along with funds from royal events and donations, he set up his first charity, The Prince's Trust. The Prince wanted the charity to help disadvantaged young people in the UK, especially those in towns and cities, who felt left out or left behind. With unemployment going up, the charity's aim was to give young people guidance and skills, and develop their talents, in a way that would help prepare them for life. The Prince was passionate about his charity. He threw himself into fundraising, and it was soon drawing in millions of pounds.

But, as heir to the throne, it wasn't enough for Charles to think about his own role in life – he also needed to think about marriage. And the pressure was growing stronger all the time.

When Charles reached his 30th birthday, in November 1978, that pressure reached a peak. The newspapers were full of speculation and stories about any woman he was seen or photographed with, but Charles wasn't yet ready to get married.

Back in 1970, Charles had met a young woman named Camilla Shand at a polo match. They had started dating before Charles went to serve in the Royal Navy. But, by the time he returned, Camilla was engaged to someone else. Unable to marry the person he most wanted, Charles turned to his great-uncle, Lord Mountbatten, for help. He was advised by his great-uncle to

A young Prince Charles relaxes after a polo match with Camilla Shand (as she was then known).

Prince Charles had always been close to Lord Mountbatten. This photo, taken in 1954, shows them playing together on the beach in Malta. Princess Anne is with Mountbatten's wife, Edwina.

choose, "a suitable... and sweet-charactered girl."

In 1979, however, Charles lost his most trusted adviser. That summer, Mountbatten was in Ireland, with his daughter and her family. On August 27, they took a fishing trip on the family boat. They hadn't gone far when a bomb exploded, blowing up the boat, killing Mountbatten, his grandson, his daughter's mother-in-law and a local boy, Paul Maxwell, as well as severely injuring the others.

The bomb was a terrorist attack by the Irish Republican Army (IRA), who had long been fighting to join Northern Ireland with the rest of the Republic of Ireland.

For Charles, Mountbatten's death was a huge blow. Years later, he remembered him as "the grandfather I never had" who was always there to give him wise advice.

Mountbatten's death left Charles raw and vulnerable, and in need of someone to turn to.

Prince Charles, relaxed and smiling, with his great-uncle, Lord Mountbatten, after watching a polo match at Windsor. The photograph is from July, 1979.

Lady Diana Spencer and Prince Charles posing for a photograph after the announcement of their engagement on February 24, 1981

Chapter 4

Marriage

Not long after, Charles was staying at a friend's house in Sussex, at the same time as the nineteen-year-old Lady Diana Spencer. Their paths had crossed a few times before, but this time their meeting led to a romance.

Still in shock after Mountbatten's death, Charles, under growing pressure to get married, thought he had finally met the "suitable" and "sweet-charactered girl" that Mountbatten had urged him to find.

Over the next few months, Charles and Diana mostly stayed in touch through telephone calls. After meeting just thirteen times, Charles proposed and Diana immediately accepted. On February 24, 1981, Buckingham Palace announced their engagement.

Prince Charles and Lady Diana at Balmoral, in May, 1981, during their engagement

Just over five months later, Charles and Diana were married at St. Paul's Cathedral, in a wedding ceremony watched by 750 million people around the world. Described as a fairytale wedding, Charles wore the uniform of a naval commander while Diana dressed in an ivory gown, covered in lace, with a 25-foot train.

There was wonderful music and a procession of horse-drawn carriages. When they stood on the palace balcony to greet the crowds, the couple kissed and everyone erupted into cheers.

Charles and Diana on their wedding day, July 29, 1981, on the balcony at Buckingham Palace

Diana was an instant hit with the public. When Charles and Diana went on their first trip to Wales together, in October 1981, the crowds began chanting, "We want Diana!"

Everyone loved how warm and approachable Diana was, and she was soon overshadowing Charles at public events, which Charles couldn't help but mind. She was incredibly elegant, too, and the press constantly wrote about her looks, often comparing her wardrobe to Charles' much more old-fashioned clothes.

Even in the very early days of their marriage, the relationship between Charles and Diana was often difficult. They had hardly known each other before they got married, and soon discovered they had very few interests in common.

However, they had the birth of their first child to look forward to. Prince William was born on June 21, 1982, and unlike his father before him, Prince Charles was at his wife's side throughout. Afterwards, Charles wrote to a friend that William's birth, "meant more to me that I could ever have imagined."

A baby Prince William sits on his father's lap beside his mother, Princess Diana, at their home in Kensington Palace.

Charles and Diana both adored their son and wanted to be more present in his life than their own parents had been in theirs. At nine months old, William came with them on a royal tour of Australia and New Zealand. When they were alone together as a family, Charles wrote that they were extremely happy.

Crowds of well-wishers reach out to greet
Charles and Diana in Queensland, Australia.

But Diana was struggling with the strain of life in the public eye and the never-ending attention of the press. Her mental health was suffering, and Charles didn't know what to do.

On September 15, 1984, Charles and Diana's second child, Prince Henry, was born, known to everyone as Harry. Again, Charles was delighted, writing, "how different a character he is from William," and marvelling at his "long and slender" fingers.

This photograph shows Charles and Diana, on board the Royal Yacht *Britannia*, reunited with their children after being away on a tour of Venice.

Here, Charles and Diana are in the Isles of Scilly in June, 1989, with their two children, Prince William and Prince Harry.

Charles loved playing with his boys, reading to them and being there for bath time. All the while, however, Charles and Diana were growing further apart. It was a hugely unhappy time for them both. Charles and Diana threw themselves into their charity work, with Diana focusing on AIDS charities and raising awareness of landmines, while Charles also worked on turning his estate, Highgrove, into an organic farm.

45

Charles and Diana on a tour of South Korea in November, 1992; they announced their separation a month later.

By 1986, Charles and Diana were living separate lives. The Royal Family didn't approve of divorce and Prince Charles thought that as heir to the throne, and future head of the Church of England, it wouldn't be possible for them to separate. It was becoming clear to everyone, however, that their marriage was unhappy. It was summed up in a famous photograph, taken in 1992 during a royal tour of India, showing Diana alone by the Taj Mahal, a building designed as a symbol of love.

Princess Diana sitting outside the Taj Mahal, in February, 1992

That year was a very difficult one for the royal family. Prince Andrew announced that he was separating from his wife while, a month later, Princess Anne announced that she was divorcing her husband. In June, a newspaper started publishing extracts from a new book about Princess Diana, which blamed Charles for Diana's difficult time in their marriage. Charles decided he wanted to put across *his* side of the story through a biography and on television.

A photograph capturing Prince Charles' television interview with Jonathan Dimbleby, broadcast on June 29, 1994

The Queen's anguish was added to by a fire at Windsor Castle, one of her most beloved homes, and the announcement, in December, that Charles and Diana were going to separate.

Prince Charles was now a far less popular figure than Diana and support for him began to plummet. He couldn't help wondering what the future might hold.

Here you can see Windsor Castle going up in flames, on November 20, 1992. The fire destroyed 115 rooms, including nine State Rooms.

Chapter 5

Tragedy and hope

After Charles and Diana's divorce, their relationship started to get better. They would meet up to talk about the children and went to school events together.

That summer, Diana was away in France while Charles, William and Harry, along with the Queen and Prince Philip, were at Balmoral. It was a happy and relaxed place for them, where Charles

Prince Charles with Prince William, 15, and Harry, 12, taking an early morning walk by the river at Balmoral, on August 12, 1997

Princess Diana with her sons, enjoying the rides at an amusement park in August, 1993; she wanted her sons to have as normal an upbringing as possible.

had taught the boys to fish and they could have quiet time together. But their peace was shattered on the morning of August 31, 1997. Charles was woken to be told that Diana had died, in the early hours of the morning, in a car accident in Paris.

One of the first people he called was his adviser, Julia Cleverdon. Her husband had died just two weeks earlier and she'd had to break the news to her daughters, who were similar in age to William and Harry. "What do you say to children?" Charles asked. "How do you explain this?"

Charles told the boys what had happened, and then, leaving them in the care of their grandparents, he flew to Paris to bring back Diana's body.

Diana's sisters, Jane and Sarah, flew with him. All three were overcome with grief. "It all seems unreal," Charles said to the British ambassador.

Their sadness was felt by the public, too. Huge crowds flocked to Kensington Palace in London, where Diana had lived, leaving mountains of gifts, notes and flowers. Such a massive outpouring of public grief had never been seen before.

At the funeral, Charles walked in procession with his sons, behind the coffin. Then Charles and the boys went together to Highgrove.

Flowers left by mourners outside Kensington Palace in the days following Princess Diana's funeral, in September, 1997

Prince Charles (far right) walking with his sons at Diana's funeral, with Prince Philip (far left) and Princess Diana's brother (middle)

Later, Prince Harry described how their father was there for them and that he tried to make sure the boys were protected.

At Charles' first public outing, in Manchester, he said how proud he was of William and Harry. One woman shook his hand, saying, "Keep your chin up," and Charles replied with, "That's very kind of you, but I feel like crying."

Charles felt very grateful for the warm way the crowds in Manchester responded to him. Later that year, on a trip to South Africa with Harry, he took the opportunity to celebrate Diana's life.

He talked about the "real difference" her work had brought to so many lives, from raising awareness of AIDS to the need to ban landmines, and he spoke of the tragedy of her death.

Prince Charles and his sons, William and Harry, on a skiing trip together in Klosters, Switzerland

Charles did his best to support his sons as they were growing up, in a world without their mother. They both went to boarding school, to Eton College, where the Queen Mother had once wanted Charles to go. There were summers in Scotland, Christmases at the royal estate, Sandringham, and bonding over foxhunting and polo. When it was time for Prince William to go to university, Charles was there like any other parent, carrying his son's bags to his room.

At the same time, Charles kept up his devoted work to his charities, as well as his royal duties. His main charity, The Prince's Trust, had been growing ever since Charles had first started it, in 1976. The Trust held its first rock concert in Hyde Park as a fundraising event, and began providing mentors for teenagers who had been in care. It set up a scheme for young offenders, as well as clubs to help disadvantaged teenagers.

Prince Charles also pursued his passion for architecture, with a town-planning project in Poundbury, Dorset. Building began in 1993, and Charles made sure that the new buildings were all in a traditional style, with the aim of creating an attractive place for people to live and work.

He became involved, too, in a project in Scotland, rescuing an 18th-century house, so that it could stay open to the public.

A photograph of Dumfries House, in Scotland, which opened its doors for the first time in 250 years in 2008, after being saved by Prince Charles.

Charles kept on speaking out about everything from farming to saving old buildings to caring for the environment. But he caused an uproar with his speeches against modern British architecture and genetically modified crops, and all the letters he wrote to politicians. As Prince of Wales, he was allowed to voice his opinions, but he was criticized in the press for going too far.

As time went on, however, Charles was praised for his views on the environment. In 2011, he was invited to speak at a summit on climate change. "It is very simple: we must save our forests," he said, highlighting the "critical challenges" we face without them. He was fast becoming a powerful voice on protecting the natural world.

As people's understanding of Prince Charles began to change, so, too, did his personal life. In February 2005, it was announced that Prince Charles was engaged to be married again, to his first love, Camilla. Her own marriage had ended in divorce and they had always remained close.

The wedding took place in April with Prince William, and Camilla's son, as witnesses. Out of respect for Diana, Camilla took the title of the Duchess of Cornwall, rather than Princess of Wales.

Charles and
Camilla on
their wedding
day at Windsor
Guildhall

The public's support for Charles and the rest of the royal family was also improving. Prince Harry had joined the army after leaving school and, though anxious for his son, Charles was also very proud of him fighting on the front line in Afghanistan.

After university, Prince William joined the Royal Air Force, where he stayed for seven years, before leaving to take on more charity work. In 2011, he married Catherine Middleton, whom he had met at university.

Prince William and Prince Harry at RAF Shawbury on June 18, 2009, while both were on their military helicopter training courses

The spectacular wedding ceremony, at Westminster Abbey, was watched by nearly three billion people around the world.

William and Catherine ride in a carriage on their wedding day.

By this time, both Charles' sons were taking on more royal duties, with Prince Harry setting up the Invictus Games in 2014, using sports to inspire and support wounded, injured and sick servicemen and women. William, Harry and Catherine also worked together on a mental health charity, Heads Together.

Prince Harry, Catherine (then known as the Duchess of Cambridge) and Prince William attending an event in support of Heads Together

In 2011, Charles reached a milestone. He became the longest-serving heir to the British throne, having broken Edward VII's record of sixty years. But he was as busy and committed as ever to his role. "He never, ever stops working," Camilla commented.

US President Barack Obama meeting Prince Charles in the Oval Office, The White House, on May 4, 2011

The Queen, at this time, was more popular than ever. In 2012, she celebrated her Diamond Jubilee, marking her sixty years on the throne. Her incredibly long reign meant that for many she was the only monarch they had ever known. The Prince praised her in his speech: "Your

The Queen and Prince Philip, in 2011, opening a laboratory at the University of Cambridge, being greeted by flag-waving crowds.

Majesty... Mummy..." he began, drawing cheers from the crowds, before thanking her, "for making us proud to be British."

All through her eighties, the Queen didn't seem to be slowing down. In 2012 she did 424 public engagements to the Prince's 480.

In 2016, however, when the Queen was reaching her ninetieth birthday, she began handing over more of her duties to Charles. He was receiving government documents as well as taking on more public roles. And he was to take on more, still, after the death of his father, Prince Philip, in 2021, at the age of ninety-nine.

As a young boy, Prince Charles had looked up to his father. At times their relationship had been difficult, partly because they were so different. In a 2016 interview, Prince Philip had said: "Charles is a romantic — and I am a pragmatist" — and went on to describe how that meant they often saw things differently.

Over the years, however, they had grown much closer, discovering they shared many interests, from painting and wildlife to supporting charities that focused on young people.

After his father's death, Charles spoke of his loss. "My family and I miss my father enormously," he said. And without her "strength and stay" — as the Queen had described her husband — she began to rely more than ever on Charles.

Prince Charles with his father, Prince Philip, in 2016, in Poundbury, Dorset

Prince Charles takes on the duty of reading the Queen's Speech in May, 2022, at the State Opening of Parliament.

Chapter 6

Becoming King

Following the death of his father, Charles took on more of his mother's duties. He acted as her official consort to the State Opening of Parliament in 2021 and read the Queen's Speech for the first time in 2022. But as Charles was stepping up, his younger son, Prince Harry, decided to step down as a senior royal.

In 2018, Prince Harry had married Meghan Markle, an American actor. Much of the public had been hugely excited, seeing Meghan, who is biracial, as a symbol of the modern royal family. Meghan, however, struggled with constant negative press attention from the British media, and

Harry and Meghan arriving at the Royal Albert Hall in London, in 2020

Prince Harry didn't want to see her suffer, as his own mother had done. The couple made the decision to move first to Canada, before settling in the USA.

As Meghan and Harry spoke out about their difficult time as part of the royal family, Harry and Charles became more and more distant, as did Harry and William. Charles felt very saddened and missed his son deeply.

The year 2022, however, began as a year of celebration, with the Platinum Jubilee, marking the Queen's reign of seventy years. There was

Charles, with Camilla at his side, celebrates the Queen's life during the BBC Platinum Party at the Palace on June 4, 2022.

a Service of Thanksgiving, and fires were lit up and down the country, followed by a "Party at the Palace" – a televised night of musical tributes. At the end of the concert, the Prince celebrated his mother's reign. "You laugh and cry with us," he said, "and, most importantly, you have been there for us, for these seventy years."

Buckingham Palace was turned into a huge concert venue for the Platinum Jubilee "Party at the Palace." Here, the rock band Duran Duran perform in front of a crowd of thousands.

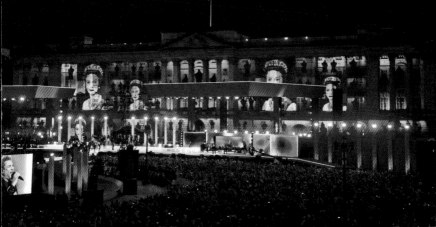

After the Jubilee, the Queen went to one of her most-loved places, Balmoral. She was growing noticeably frailer and on September 8, she died, peacefully, with her eldest children, Charles and Anne, by her side.

The whole world responded to the Queen's death. Royals, leaders, and celebrities from across the globe spoke about how much she had meant to them. "In a world of constant change, she was a steadying presence..." said US President Biden, while in Britain, more than 250,000 waited in line to see the Queen's lying-in-state in Westminster Hall.

The moment the Queen died, the throne passed immediately to Charles, who was officially proclaimed King two days later, at an event at St. James's Palace in London.

It must have been a strange time for Charles. Full of grief, as his beloved mother had died, while knowing, in that same moment, he had finally become King. He would have to give up many things he had loved – he could no longer speak out about all the issues that mattered to him, or be so involved in his many charities. But looking back at his nearly seventy years as heir to the throne, he had so much to be proud of. His Prince's Trust charity had helped more than one million unemployed and disadvantaged young people since its launch almost fifty years ago.

Plans for the Coronation, code-named Operation Golden Orb, began immediately. The date was fixed for May 6, 2023, when Charles would formally be crowned at Westminster Abbey, alongside Camilla.

Here Charles is publicly proclaimed King by the Governor of the Tower of London. Behind him stands the King's Guard and the Yeomen of the Guard.

The day itself dawned with mist and drizzle. Undeterred, all along The Mall, in London, thousands of royal fans had camped overnight to catch a glimpse of the King and Queen Consort, on their way to Westminster Abbey.

Charles and Camilla left Buckingham Palace in "The King's Procession" – in a gilded, horse-drawn carriage, accompanied by troops and military bands. The King waved at the crowds, but his expression was serious and solemn.

Inside the Abbey, over 2,000 guests were waiting, including royals and heads of state from around the world, famous celebrities and everyday heroes, while millions more watched on television.

At Westminster Abbey, the King kneels to take his oath and prays to be "a blessing for all... of every faith and belief."

A very symbolic moment – King Charles sits in the Coronation Chair, as the Archbishop of Canterbury places the crown on his anointed head.

The Abbey was described by one guest as "like being inside a jewel box" – full of candlelight and glowing with gold. Music, from choirs, orchestras and soloists, swelled to the rafters.

During the ancient ceremony, the King swore an oath, then his Robes of State were removed. He was shielded by screens before being anointed with holy oil. Then came the crowning moment – the Archbishop placed the solid gold St. Edward's Crown on the King's head. The Abbey bells rang for two minutes, trumpets sounded and gun salutes were fired across the UK.

The King moved to his throne where the Prince of Wales pledged his loyalty and kissed his father's cheek. Then it was Camilla's turn to be anointed and crowned.

The King and Queen return to the palace in the Gold State Coach.

After the Service, the royal family gathered on Buckingham Palace balcony to wave to the cheering crowds, even as the rain kept falling. Overhead, RAF planes known as the Red Arrows zoomed across the sky in a blaze of red, white and blue.

The following day there was a star-studded Coronation Concert at Windsor Castle, including a performance by the Coronation Choir, made up of refugee choirs, NHS choirs, LGBTQ+ singing groups and deaf signing choirs.

The celebrations continued with a "Coronation Big Lunch" made up of thousands of street parties, decorated with fluttering bunting and Union Jack flags. The public were also invited to volunteer as part of "The Big Help Out" to support their local area. And after it was all over, the King and Queen said how grateful they were to everyone who took part. "We thank you, each and every one... We now rededicate our lives to serving the people of the United Kingdom, the realms and Commonwealth."

The message of the Coronation was one of celebration and coming together, of ancient tradition and modern Britain, and a King promising to serve "with loyaly, respect and love."

Charles and Camilla, wearing their crowns, wave to the crowds from the balcony of Buckingham Palace.

Photographic credits:

Cover image © Hugo Burnand/Royal Household 2023; © **Alamy** spine p25 (Trinity Mirror/Mirrorpix), p1 (PA Images), p2-3 (Rick Wood Photography), p4 (John Frost Newspapers), p5 (SuperStock), p6 (Trinity Mirror/Mirrorpix), p7 (Chronicle), p10 (PA Images), p12 (PA Images), p14 (PA Images), p24 (PA Images), p25 (Trinity Mirror/ Mirrorpix), p27 (PA Images), p29 (PA Images), p31 (b) (PA Images), p32 (PA Images), p33 (PA Images), p44 (ZUMA Press, Inc.), p45 (PA Images), p46 (David Cooper), p52 (jeremy sutton-hibbert), p54 (Anwar Hussein), p55 (allan wright), p57 (PA Images), p59 (tr) (Scott Wishart), p60 (White House Photo), p64 (Anwar Hussein), p67 (PA Images), p69 (Xinhua); © **Camera Press** p9 (PHOTOGRAPH BY CECIL BEATON, CAMERA PRESS LONDON); © **Getty Images** p8 (Popperfoto), p11 (Lisa Sheridan/Hulton Royals Collection), p13 (tr) Keystone/Hulton Royals Collection), p13 (b) (Hulton Archive), p15 (Hulton Archive/Hulton Royals Collection), p16 (Keystone-France/Gamma-Keystone), p19 (Keystone/Hulton Royals Collection), p20 (Central Press/Hulton Archive), p21 (Paul Popper/Popperfoto), p22 (Ray Bellisario/Popperfoto), p23 (Central Press/Hulton Royals Collection), p31 (t) (Popperfoto), p35 (Serge Lemoine/Hulton Royals Collection), p37 (Tim Graham), p38 (Hulton Deutsch/Corbis Historical), p39 (Mirrorpix), pp40-41 (Anwar Hussei), p42 (Tim Graham), p43 (Anwar Hussein), p49 (Tim Graham Photo Library), p50 (Anwar Hussein), p51 (Julian Parker/UK Press), p53 (AFP), p58 (Chris Jackson), p59 (WPA Pool), p61 (WPA Pool), p62 (WPA Pool), p63 (WPA Pool), p65 (t) (JONATHAN BUCKMASTER/AFP), p65 (b) (HANNAH MCKAY/AFP), p68 (WPA Pool/Pool), p70 (Dan Kitwood/Staff), p71 (OLI SCARFF/Contributor); © **Shutterstock** p48 (ITV); © **The Royal Household** p28; © **Topfoto.co.uk** p17, p18, p36.

Please note some of the black and white images in the book have been digitally tinted by Usborne.

Edited by Jane Chisholm
Digital manipulation by Keith Furnival
With thanks to Ruth King for her help with picture research

First published in 2023 by Usborne Publishing Limited, 83-85 Saffron Hill, London EC1N 8RT, United Kingdom. usborne.com Copyright © 2023 Usborne Publishing Limited.